I am JESSE JAMES

Eric Hameister ✠ Dave McClain ✠ Curtis Cummings

Viking Studio

VIKING STUDIO Published by the Penguin Group ✠ Penguin Group (USA) Inc., 375 Hudson Street, New York, New York 10014, U.S.A. ✠ Penguin Books Ltd, 80 Strand, London WC2R 0RL, England ✠ Penguin Books Australia Ltd, 250 Camberwell Road, Camberwell, Victoria 3124, Australia ✠ Penguin Books Canada Ltd, 10 Alcorn Avenue, Toronto, Ontario, Canada M4V 3B2 ✠ Penguin Books India (P) Ltd, 11 Community Centre, Panchsheel Park, New Delhi – 110 017, India ✠ Penguin Books (N.Z.) Ltd, Cnr Rosedale and Airborne Roads, Albany, Auckland, New Zealand ✠ Penguin Books (South Africa) (Pty) Ltd, 24 Sturdee Avenue, Rosebank, Johannesburg 2196, South Africa ✠ Penguin Books Ltd, Registered Offices: 80 Strand, London WC2R 0RL, England ✠ First published by Viking Studio, a member of Penguin Group (USA) Inc., 2004 ✠ Text copyright © Payupsucker, Inc., 2004 ✠ Photographs copyright © Eric Hameister, 2004 ✠ All rights reserved ✠ CIP data available ✠ ISBN 0-14-200503-7 ✠ Printed in the United Kingdom.

Concept **Jesse James** Photography **Eric Hameister** Design **Dave McClain** Text **Curtis Cummings** Art Direction **Jaye Zimet** Production **Grazyna Veras** Editorial **Jennifer Ehmann** Managing Editorial **Tory Klose** Printing **Butler & Tanner Ltd**

1 3 5 7 9 10 8 6 4 2

"You know those needlepoint wall hangings that say 'Home Sweet Home'? I just had my friend's mom, who is really good at those, make one for my house. It says 'Go F--- Yourself,' but it looks exactly like a nice needlepoint."

West Coast Choppers' world headquarters sits in a ragged South Bay neighborhood known for gangs and graffiti. CHOPPERS FOR LIFE is tagged across the building in razor-sharp barrio script. It's a place Jesse James calls home.

"I grew up in an all-Mexican neighborhood. I was born in Lynwood, California, and grew up in South Gate. I've been buying Dickies and Pendelton's at the same clothing store my whole life. My dad shopped there when he was a kid. I've been dressing the same way since I was twelve. It's just who I am."

INTRODUCTION

In the 1970s Jesse's Long Beach stomping grounds rattled and shook as metalworkers flogged their homemade choppers to the nearby navy shipyards and defense plants. The endless demand for machinists, fabricators, and welders meant that Long Beach was a kind of hotbed for choppers and bikers. A lot of open garages on residential streets and in the surrounding communities spewed out sparks deep into the night, as long-haired chopper freaks turned four-hundred-dollar ex-cop bikes into stretched-out spindly street machines. Sometimes it seemed like half of South Bay was shaking to the thump of Harley-Davidson pistons. The rumbling stripped-skinny customs burned an impression on kid Jesse.

Weaned on California Cool, dirt bikes, skateboards, low riders, Hot Wheels, and punk rock, Jesse accepted and rejected opposing influences and inspirations and developed a desire to make things better through his own handiwork. His appreciation for custom fabrication was taking shape. "It wasn't Kustom Kulture, as a kid. I remember the Cars of the Stars, and Planes of Fame, next to Knott's Berry Farm. My dad drove to work between Long Beach and San Bernardino on the 91 freeway, and when we'd come up on Knott's I'd have my face glued to the window of his truck, hoping I could see a custom car or bike parked in the parking lot. That's where Von Dutch worked. This was all through the seventies. I remember going to shows at Long Beach Sports Arena and seeing just bitchin' shit. I mean, car shows were so much crazier than they are now. Now everything is subtle and sanitary and clean—they're great cars but they used to be so exaggerated with the candy paint and the crazy motors, they were just sensory overload. I loved anything custom, like cars with giant huge motors. They obviously didn't work or run. It was just dumb, but I loved that."

Jesse was also inspired by his father. "When I was real young, you know my dad was in the antiques business, and I watched him take furniture, mainly barber chairs and stuff like that, and he'd take rusted shitty ones and restore them and make them cool. I picked up some good knowledge about refinishing stuff. I can refinish old furniture today and I think that that process, the taking of something really shitty and making it really beautiful or fully restored, that feeling was there with me from way back. Then I started doing bicycles and beach cruisers, and I was still really young. I'm addicted to the process where if you take something and you really don't know how it's gonna look but when it's done and painted and chromed, and every piece you put on it, it starts to look better and better and better, then *wham!* It's all done and looks right, and you're just so satisfied at how it came out."

Like most mechanically gifted craftsmen, Jesse remembers from a young age disassembling things around the house and then meticulously reassembling them. From early on, he was unconsciously wiring his brain for what was later to come. "I was a pretty regular kid. I was full of anger and hate, you know, in my teens, but as a young kid I really didn't hate too much. Just my sister and some kid named Steven down the street."

From his father's example in careful restoration to the music he grew up listening to, Jesse's orbit has always revolved around the concept of "I can do this myself without any need for outside help because I believe in myself." He spent endless hours alone perfecting his skills. That kind of solitary dedication and self-confidence made him a bit of an outsider, and he gravitated toward others like him. "We were all kind of punk rockers around here. I started going to punk shows when I was eleven and they're the best memories I have as a kid."

Only a few years later, with the western sun on his back and the Dead Kennedys pounding in his ears, Jesse the teenager took torch to metal and never looked back. He looked at the outright lameness of the then-trendy body panels and peach paint jobs and knew he could do better. Where was the menace? Where were the bikes that growled, "Get the f--- away from me or I'll napalm your home town"? Why should you have to look backward to get a cool stripped-down chopper with a bad attitude? It was time to knock the custom bike world into the future.

While still working as a part-time bodyguard, Jesse launched his attack on the chopper world and opened a small shop in the LBC. His visions transmuted into radical choppers that shouted, "Look! This is what you're missing. This is how I'm gonna do it, how it should be done, and how it's always supposed to have been done. I'm gonna reel all you clueless jokers in and learn ya a thing or two." In the beginning, the custom bike establishment met Jesse with slack-jawed dismissal. "Nobody would want a bike that extreme," they said with contempt. "That kid's goin' nowhere." But Jesse knew the obvious rightness of his ideas.

Over the years he would learn to take classic chopper elements and refine them to create total-performance machines that make an extreme statement. He improved every aspect of every component—junked all extraneous detail, created perfect welds and clever design elements—resulting in bikes with balls-out performance and vicious curb appeal. The finished package would make the old guys in the neighborhood who had worked behind a welder's mask for fifty years stop and think, "Shit, this kid knows what he's doin'." Jesse's sensibilities absolutely bleed tradition while rewriting the book.

It took some time, but eventually everybody else caught on to the West Coast method. Before the television shows and celebrity, the creations of West Coast Choppers had already proved what Jesse had insisted on all along: Power, attitude, and quality are what make a custom truly badass. Rumors spread about the crazy motherf----- in Long Beach. His ultrapricey handbuilts started getting magazine attention. Suddenly there was a waiting list twenty bikes deep. Then fifty. The shop shifted into overdrive, and the new ideas and engineering breakthroughs came fast—the pace has never let up.

Jesse's maverick personality is perfectly suited to a media constantly in search of something different, and the world has become as interested in the man as his mission. Not bad for an ex-bodyguard from Lynwood. "I think I give people more than they're expecting: doing bikes the right way regardless of the price and giving them more than they think they're gonna get. So when they pick up their bike it's full of hidden shit—they look under their oil tank and it says F--- YOU. I'm unwilling to compromise. If my name and West Coast Choppers are on the tank, everything's gotta be the best."

It's about having the raw talent to come up with something that actually works and the brazenness it takes to make the world take notice. "Choppers for Life" ain't just some snappy slogan. Some still snivel, but not even Jesse's worst critics can deny the stellar build quality of his bikes and the ingenuity of the components. And then there's his attitude. It's my way. F--- you if you don't like it. And if you do like it, f--- you too.

Since Jesse hit the television screen with a barely controlled four-gear burnout across the motorhead landscape, everyone else has been trying to tag him with some kind of identity. "Every girl says she f----- me, every guy says he knows me, and everybody has some story about my being a dope dealer and starting this with drug money."

This is the story: "I just worked hard. I toured with bands half the year and the rest of it I was working in a bar at night and working on bikes during the day. People see me now and they missed all the in-between. The struggling."

You can't draw a bead on him. You can't nail him down. He ignited a chopper revolution, burning from Long Beach to Laconia. He did it with talent, dedication, and a hell of a lot of sixteen-hour days.

Everyone thinks that theirs is the best generation. But right here, right now is the best time ever for bikers and choppers. Technology has caught up to creativity. Custom bikes are wilder and better than was ever possible before. The hot-rod ethic is spreading.

And the epicenter of this revolution is a little ole chopper shop in Long Beach.

THE BIKES

"I stuck to my guns and stuck to what I liked and forced everyone to change."

– J.J.

West Coast Choppers look different. In a swarm of motorcycles, they stand apart. The first thing that hits you is their radical stance. Instead of inviting, they look uncomfortable, stripped down, like old race bikes with their mechanicals exposed. Even with their high "ape-hanger" bars, they maintain a sleek profile. They don't roll down the highway so much as attack it. Unlike other choppers that have absurdly extended forks and gas tanks up in the clouds, Jesse James's bikes are low down and threatening. One thing is immediately clear: These are not cruisers. A West Coast Chopper asserts itself from a distance without novelty. It demands respect. Everything about it growls, "Approach with caution."

Jesse hears the same thing from all of his customers. "I knew it was gonna be cool and all, but that bike changed me. It altered my way of thinking."

Carving a road on any motorcycle is an exhilarating experience that takes the rider out of the box and into the air and the weather and the noise. The senses are magnified, and even on the best day with the least traffic buzzing around, they seem dangerous. Jesse's choppers push this experience further—every brain cell pops into overdrive. Instead of climbing onto one of his bikes, a rider steps into it. It's low to the ground and intimidating to everyone, even to the rider. When its motor fires, fist-size pistons pulse in an explosive tommy-gun beat. The asphalt grinds by, only inches under the bike, like a massive endless belt sander. The open primary belt spins crazily at your heel, daring you to slide just a little farther back . . . another half inch and it'll rip that Converse High-Top to shreds and cough out the ragged canvas. At the end of the ride, with a couple hundred miles' worth of these hypersensations pulsing through the brain,

the West Coast Chopper rider emerges, changed. And he can never go back.

By definition, every chopper is unique, or it should be. Like clothing and hairstyles, each chopper fits its individual owner. Traditionally, alterations have always been trial and error, their base engineering evolving in a grassroots way—out of sweat and welding torches, not slide rules and metallurgy charts. The nature of a custom bike demands that some educated—and a lot of uneducated—guesswork is involved. Even the most carefully assembled customs have been cursed with broken components, seized engines, and detaching bodywork. And nothing kills a weekend quicker than a dead chopper two hundred miles from home.

For his lucky customers, Jesse takes the guesswork away. He sweats every tiny detail so the buyer can pick up his bike and shoot off into the unknown with no fear of broken welds or mysterious steering geometry. Jesse builds both rigid and sprung frames propelled by wacky big motors that run straight out of the gate. Like a spoiled heiress, these bikes are uncontrollable, wild, and hungry for kicks.

Jesse's first real custom build started as a basket-case shovelhead. This worn-out mess of parts became a first-rate custom, and made a lot of people aware of him for the first time. In retrospect, that shovel chopper was a kind of early design platform for what would eventually evolve into the West Coast Choppers CFL (Choppers for Life) bikes.

That old shovelhead meant a lot to Jesse. "There's something about an S&S motor. When I first had a bike, to have an S&S stroker motor made in Viola, Wisconsin, and you could picture George Smith, the guy who started it. . . ." Always aware of the roots from which his vision of two-wheeled mayhem sprang, Jesse can relate to Smith's efforts to squeeze every bit of power possible from the old engines. "Nothing sounds like a 98 stroker shovel."

It may seem like West Coast Choppers happened overnight, but years of ups and downs and endless hours in the shop perfecting every aspect of the bikes went into making it what it is today. It developed gradually and cleverly over time to the Strip 'em and stroke 'em tradition, but refined to a new, unheard-of level. As Jesse puts it: "All my bikes are F--- You bikes."

Before Jesse James burned his massive skid mark across the bleached boxers of chopperdom, custom bikes had taken a bad turn from the skinny street machines of the classic chopper profile to pastel paint jobs, goofy bodywork, and tasteless chrome. Nonthreatening graphics and softly sprung rides were pushing customs into palatability and more mainstream acceptance. Cuteness somehow elbowed itself into the chopper culture. In some sort of mass delusion, these overweight barges became what the public seemed to want.

Jesse had other ideas. Bikes should be kick-start-only rigids with tiny unpadded seats and a stance that growls "Keep the f--- away from me." Their rubber-shredding torque makes the tires wish they had never been molded, and their twisted, uncorked pipes set off every car alarm for blocks. Jesse uses bigger, stronger frame tubes and demands solid handling that doesn't shimmy at speed or over rough roads. They are thin but not frail. These are definitely not bikes a mother-in-law would want a ride on. One of Jesse's mottoes is: "If you don't look like a f------ badass riding it, why do it?" Like the movie says, "Build it and they will come." Jesse built and they came. But not right away.

What seems so clear now was a hard sell to a public whose eyes had been trained to expect something else. Something lesser.

"Some guys like those big beach bars with their feet out, and they're like 'Oooh, I'm riding!' And to me that's just lame."

Jesse's bikes are about taking risks, and that philosophy applies to building them, riding them, and selling them. "I did what I really wanted whether it was marketable or sellable or not. Everybody else, I think, kind of did bikes that people would like to buy and pay for them to customize. And I did bikes that, well, I went to Daytona for, like, eight straight years and didn't sell a f------ thing. No one bought my bikes. I think they thought they were neat to look at but nobody would plunk down the money. All I heard was sniveling: 'Oooh, that looks uncomfortable' or 'That's only kick-start,' or 'I don't know about a rigid, you know, that'll hurt your back.' And I loved it. It affected business a lot, but I stuck to my guns and stuck to what I liked and forced everyone to change." Not only change, but also copy shamelessly. Radical Hell Bent Pipes have become an industry standard and now are mimicked by multiple manufacturers.

Jesse builds his choppers to be thrashed, and he tests his designs through his own relentless abuse. Rigid frames, always known for flex under power, went from squirrelly to scary with the new big-inch motors bolted in. Designed for 40 horsepower Panhead motors, they just couldn't cope acceptably with the new breed of monster 100+ horsepower power plants. Because Jesse began using engines that were more powerful than any other bike builder was using, he had to build his frames from bigger tubes to tame the brutal horsepower. Not only do they provide the added strength that is needed but they also look better, more muscular.

Predictable handling is something else Jesse extracts from his creations. Designing an aggressive profile that won't pitch off the rider in an extreme situation was tackled early on. "To me, if you're gonna redo something and you don't make it better, then why bother. I like my bikes with good turning radiuses, so we raise up the bottom tubes so you corner good on the El Diablo. They're lighter, faster, and quicker handling." He continues, "There's a lot of people that build choppers just for the extremeness and the long front ends and the steering geometry. That's a little f----- up. They're neat to look at and everything, but what I like is a bike that looks like there's not enough parts there to make it run. Everything is gone except for just the necessities: motor, trans, frame, wheels, tires, front end, handlebars, a little gas tank and that's it. I had a rigid once that just had a flannel shirt wrapped around the frame 'cause I could never find a seat that I liked, so I just wrapped the shirt and sat on the frame and I rode it for five years like that."

Building a high-end client bike takes more than making a list of required components. It has to fit the owner—his character as well as his body size. But Jesse is partial to a specific look in his personal bikes. "It's just that minimalist look, kind of like a big overgrown Sportster with a giant engine in it. And choppers just should be nimble. And a bike shouldn't look complete until the rider is on it. The lines shouldn't be complete."

Jesse takes pride not only in his success as a custom bike builder, but also as a manufacturer of frames, tanks, fenders, and other components. But if Levi Strauss and Co. can't make it in America anymore, how can West Coast Choppers do it? "I think that we've gotten so wrapped up in computers and technology and pricing and stuff like that that I think it's worth the extra two dollars to have it made by Americans. But people don't see it that way. It's all about cost and saving a nickel. I've always priced my stuff more, a little bit higher, but I try to give them a little bit extra. Give 'em more than their money's worth but not get into price wars with other people. And it seems to work."

A West Coast Chopper requires commitment. If posing is your main interest, do yourself a favor and keep on looking. These are riders' bikes and it takes more than a love of flash to commit to eating up the miles of uncertain urban landscape on what is not a soft ride. "Well, you have to break in the motor, but the rider has to be broken in too. You have to get down your style and riding position on these. You can't go into a coma and watch the birds fly. You gotta watch the road and steer around the big bumps. To me it's better because you're so focused on the riding and dicing in and out of traffic and stuff like that that you're mind is totally focused. When you aggressively ride you can't think of anything else or you'll f--- up. You have to pay attention and look way far ahead. I like my feet down because I ride kind of like an idiot, so I like it that if someone is gonna pull out in front of me, I'm ready. You know, the riding position."

Jesse's attitude is if riders want a relaxed riding position, if they think looking like they're on a rolling La-Z-Boy recliner is the way to be, they should look for something less demanding, like a tricycle. Better yet, maybe they should just buy the recliner and stay at home watching old episodes of *Friends*.

West Coast Choppers distill something more pure out of their owners. Attitudes are altered and nothing is ever quite the same. "A lot of bikes being built are just deluded and outright just biting my shit. It's kind of like they're for people that don't know anything about motorcycles. I'd rather take the most hardened, seasoned fabricators and mechanics and when they look at my stuff they say, 'Wow, that's a bitchin' bike.' That, to me, is way more of a compliment."

Jesse James, media star, customizer, manufacturer, alleged folk hero, is at his core a rider. Like all true motorcycle riders, it's not something that he does; it's something that he is.

"I love to ride. You know, aside from all the chrome, shiny paint, and bullshit like that, I mean, if you can't just take it and beat the shit out of it and have fun and when you get off the freeway you're heart is beating fast and you're like, 'F---! That was bitchin'!' That's ten times better than looking at it."

For a low-production manufacturer, Jesse is in the unique position of not needing any more media hype to sell his product and his message. In spite of unbelievable demands put on his time by his multiple careers, Jesse still keeps regular hours in his shop, fabricating insane choppers and planning the next idea that will again get the custom world chattering like monkeys in a cage. "I've kind of pulled out of the motorcycle media. I haven't had a bike in a big motorcycle magazine in five years. It's all advertiser driven and I'd just rather do my own thing."

In nature, a dangerous predator that roams freely and kills at will with no natural enemies of its own is called an apex predator. If ever manmade creations could be called apex killers, they would be West Coast Choppers.

They're in a class of their own. Aggression executed in steel, chrome, and metal-flake paint.

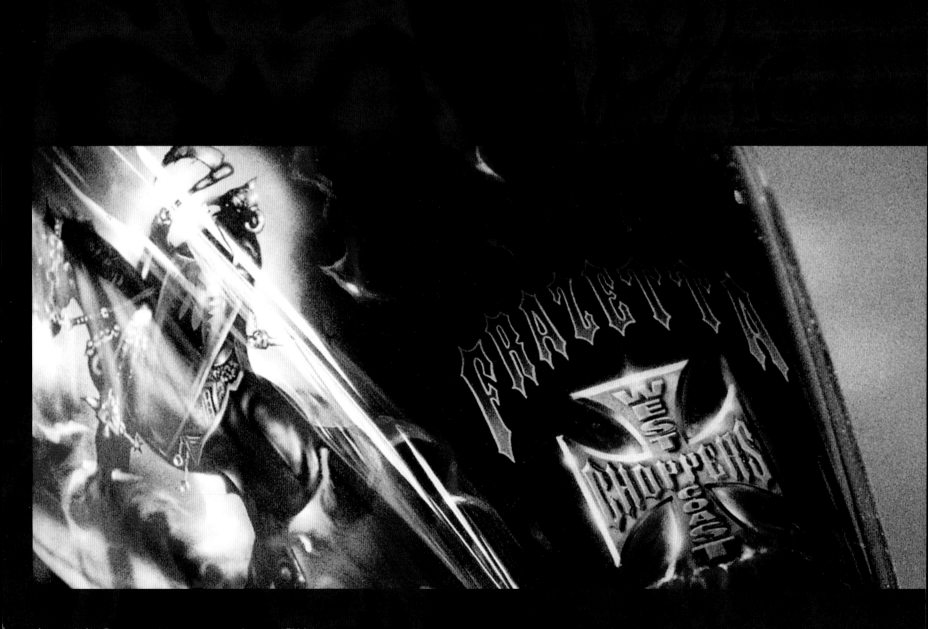

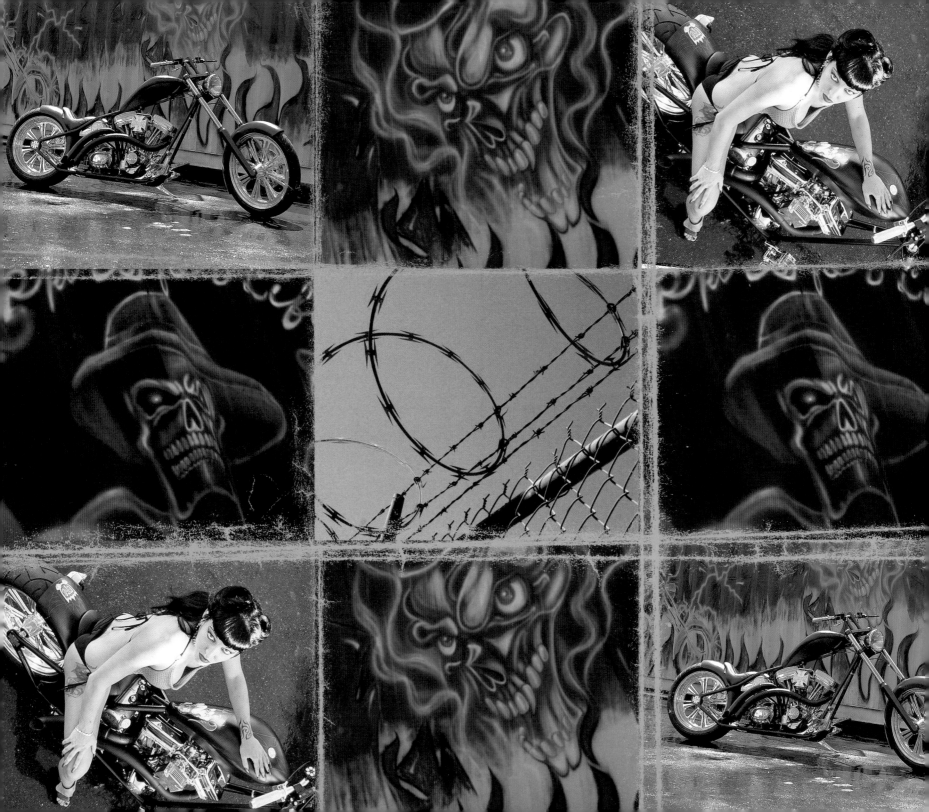

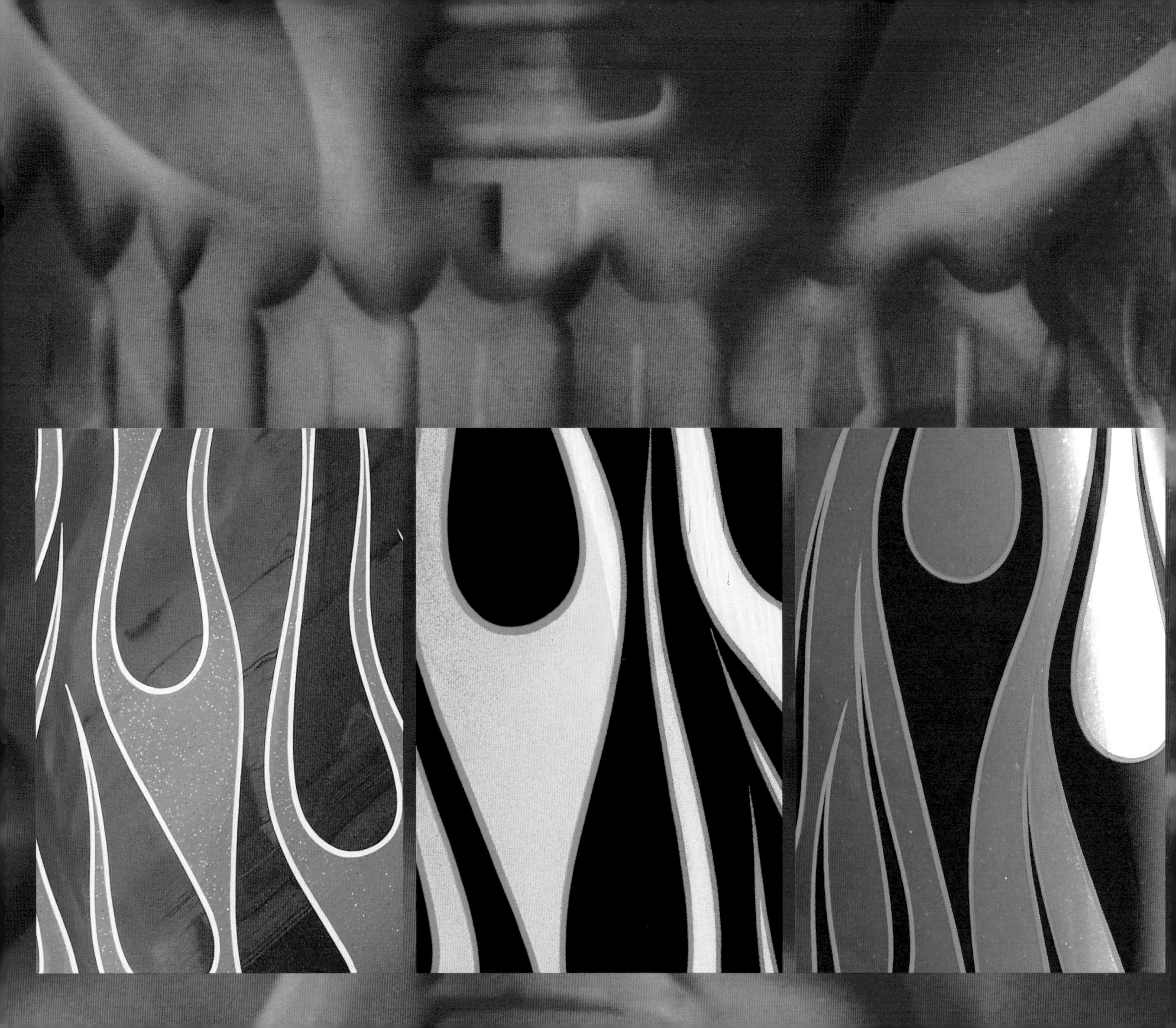

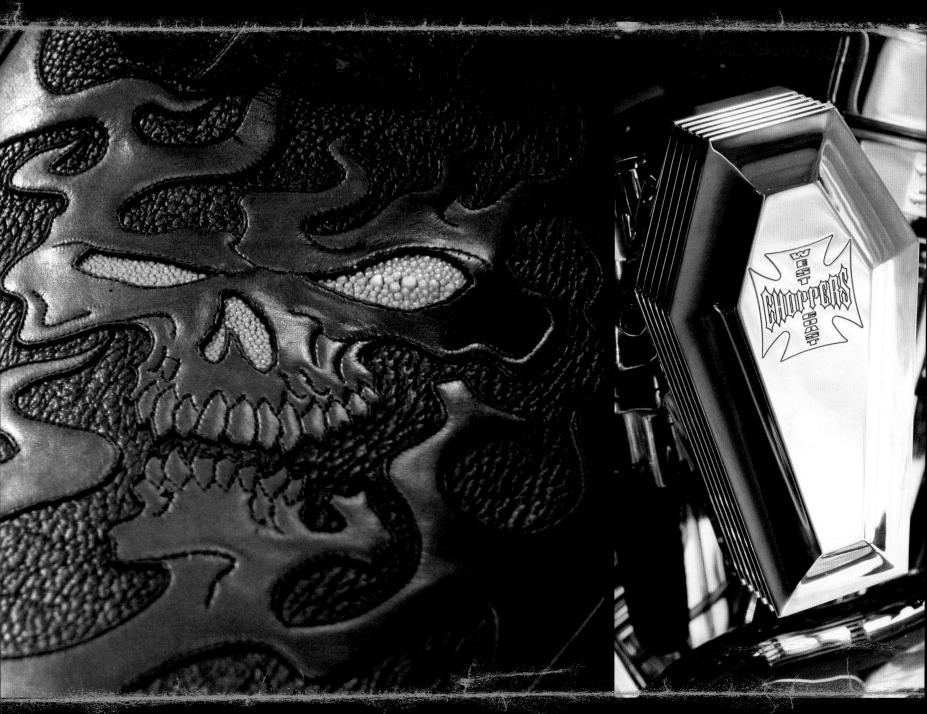

"*People who can make something with their hands could run the world.*"

– J.J.

02 > THE SHOP

It's only fitting that the West Coast Choppers headquarters butts right up against the 710 freeway, a major trucking artery from the LA harbor into downtown. It's fifteen miles of traffic, blown tires, and tractor-trailer parts kicked up by fast-moving vehicles, and it's the perfect place to shake down a new chop as hard and as fast as it will go. The locals call it the 710 shuffle: gassing the bike flat out through the heavy traffic, dodging the eighteen-wheelers, and jerking quick shimmies around the 2x4s, fallen tail lights, and pieces of metal that fly off big rigs like shrapnel.

Jesse James's California is a long way off from the sunny beach-ball dream sold to the world by television shows like *Baywatch.* The Long Beach harbor area is like any harbor area, rough and gritty and monochromatic. It's also the place where Jesse feels most connected.

Jesse's dedication to, and pride in, Long Beach is underlined every day by his choice in shop location, the Four Corners. "The Four Corners area of Long Beach is where Eastside Longos, which is a Mexican mafia gang, an Asian gang, and two Crip gangs that are north of here all come together. It's bad and it's bleak and I took a big chance seven years ago moving my stuff here, but I did it, and now I'm almost ready to pull the bars off the windows. Some of the neighborhood kids work here and there's a kind of mutual respect among all the gangs. I mean no one f---- with the shop and it's pretty good. Just being here, I feel like I'm home. I know all the cops, and all the *Monster Garage* guys have to come down from Hollywood and Burbank and the Valley. I keep the TV show here. It's my town."

And in his town, he operates the coolest clubhouse anyone's ever seen. On any given day the West Coast Choppers' showroom is packed with killer choppers, custom cars, insane *Monster Garage* vehicles, vintage racecars, and Kustom Kulture artwork. It's a museum born of King Gearhead's own twisted mind. "When I was a bodyguard, I traveled all over the world, and I went to a lot of different bike shops that I read about in magazines. But when I'd get there, it was, like, a letdown. There'd be one cool bike and then the rest was just shit. I never want that here. I want an overwhelming amount of good stuff."

As an extra attraction, the "good stuff" tends to spill out into the parking lot. The custom cars of the employees mix it up with visiting low riders, bikers, greasers, and hot-rodders. It's sort of a spontaneous, constantly cycling car show and everything good that goes with it—the posing, the tire-screeching burn-outs, and the girls on the prowl. All day long, a steady stream of camera-toting tourists pull up in minivans and rental cars. Cisco the pit-bull paces the shop floor, sniffing the fresh tires, and keeping the tourists away from where they shouldn't be.

It can sometimes be a chore for Jesse to get from his car to his office with the gauntlet of people lined up outside, each wanting a photo or a few seconds of his time. The constant intru-siveness of strangers, everyone from barrio gangsters to square john stiffs, would become annoying to even the coolest of heads. But every day, Jesse poses for pictures and signs autographs. "I was a bodyguard for a long time for a lot of famous people, and I saw them really be dicks with fans. The way I always look at it is that all of those people who come here, they're all paying my paycheck. All that money goes to bankroll the bikes and makes it so I can do what I want to do. And for a lot of them, this might be their only chance to meet me. So if I'm a dick to them, then they're gonna remember me as a dick forever. I'm just so appre-ciative of it all. It just pumps me up every day."

The stroking goes both ways. After checking out all the stuff that every motorhead dreams about, people climb into their minivans and rental cars smiling and talking excitedly, like they've just seen a really good movie.

"I like to keep a lot of cool stuff in the showroom so that when people come here, it's a good experience. There's nothing better than walking into someplace and seeing so much cool shit that you can't focus on anything. Like when you walk into this shop—well, I'm numb to it, but people walk in and it's like, whoa! Their eyes get big, the whole thing."

Inside the shop work area, beyond the showroom and cool stuff on display, beats the true heart of West Coast Choppers. In a whirlwind of thumping music, steel mesh, and glowing neon, the bikes take form. Starting with a bare metal frame, a strange voodoo is forced into the steel under the pulsing glow of an old bottle-shaped liquor sign. Their finished form still a mystery, the raw choppers line up for the delicate assembly and finishing methods. As per chopper requirements, no two end up alike.

One of the chiseled in stone rules of the WCC shop is no matter how cool the idea, if it can't be executed cleverly and work correctly, it won't be done. If a long raked-out-in-the-weeds bike is called for, it still must handle acceptably. No squirrelly shit. No flash at the expense of performance. A WCC chopper is built to ride flat out. A monster motor can't blow up. It's gotta be trick, it's gotta be custom, but it's gotta be done right. Craftily.

The ghosts of old-school metalworkers who toiled their whole lives cutting, pounding, forming, never considering their work any kind of art can be felt moving around the shop floor, around the English Wheel, the power hammers, the welding torches. "There's guys that worked right here at Douglas Aircraft in Long Beach, punchin' a clock for forty years, day in and day out, and no one ever treated them like a rock star. And it makes me humbled that I am treated like a rock star and making the money and having all the stuff, you know, for doing the same blue-collar job that they did. It keeps me grounded. I'm pretty f-----' thankful for where I am and what I have. I mean, I trip on it every day. Every single day I wake up and think, 'F---, man, I can't even believe that I'm doing this and I'm where I am.' I worked hard and achieved all of my dreams."

Jesse has always been able to surf between different worlds. His palm communicator is his constant digital link with anything and everyone, but it's hundred-year-old tools that give him what he needs to create.

"I love the power hammer—I've embraced it. Over about the last nine years, I've really gotten pretty proficient with it. I can visualize a shape and know exactly which hammer and which die to use. I love it. I guess it's like a guitar player with his favorite guitar. You know there's something about it that just feels good in his hands. I don't play music, but this is the only thing I can compare it to because you constantly have to f--- with them. You have to tune them and oil them and make sure the play is adjusted and the gap and all that. There's such a fine-tune to get that thing to hit right, and then once it's working sweet, it's just awesome. I can make anything. I love that. I mean, loading material and pressing a button has no soul."

Soul is the quotient that cannot be duplicated, and the one that is forged into every West Coast Chopper from the frame jig to completion.

"Either you're working the metal or the metal's working you. It sounds kind of weird to say this, but I think I'm better than think I am. Sometimes I make stuff and I shock myself. It's like, 'I can't believe I f-----' pulled off that shape. It's really good and perfect.' Especially when the TV show takes me away from doing so much metalwork, but then I'll come back. The other day I made a tank for James Hetfield's bike, and it came out beautiful, and I was a little taken aback by it. I didn't realize I was that good. It was a struggle, but by the end of the day, it was like, 'Wow, that really looks good.'"

For Jesse James, one of the only real negatives in being a media star is the time it robs from custom fabrication. It can be a vicious circle, because it's his abilities in the machine shop that make him, to a lot of people, more valid than most of the "personalities" that the television tends to belch out. "People who can make something with their hands could run the world."

At West Coast Choppers, in any part of the complex where someone is turning a wrench, grinding a weld, or pounding sheet metal into submission, music is blasting some kind of accompaniment. "I'm totally musically driven. You know, the 'Don't make the Vanilla Gorilla put the chrome to your dome' is a term I got from Eric Wright, Eazy-E, when I worked for him. Stuff like that stuck with me. It inspires me." The shop soundtrack is set to permanent shuffle. Speed metal, punk rock, Delta blues.

"It's very mood reflective. When I'm making a gas tank or a fender or a frame or something like that, it's like when I was riveting the copper fuel tank. There was a transition where there were sixty-three rivets on the top of it, and they were the hardest f------ rivets I've ever had to do because it was a compound curve. And getting them to line up, and hand hammering them, and making sure they set straight, and sealed and tight. . . . There was a point about halfway where it was kicking my ass. I

stopped, put on some BB King, found the perfect song, got in the groove, put my gloves back on, and just did it. I had to have the perfect song, perfect music, perfect setting, everything perfect. Then I worked, and it came out perfect. All sensory input—sight, sound, touch—has to be aligned perfectly. And then the work will come."

Every component of a Jesse James creation is assembled by hand with pride. One-of-a-kind fabricated parts means nothing is easy, and everything must be made to fit. No half-assed bullshit. No tabs breaking or welds cracking after a few hundred miles. All of this controlled chaos, creativity, and wild hi-jinx take place under the constant gaze of angels and devils and skulls and monkeys wearing fezzes. Stickers and pinstripes and graffiti tagging cover every machine, wall, and toolbox.

"If you looked at my bedroom as a kid, those Wacky Pack stickers were everywhere. And there were cars and BMX bikes and pictures and skulls and knives and guns and helmets and skateboards and everything. My room was catacombed with stuff as a kid, and that was my whole life: my bedroom and the garage. Now with my shop, it's the same thing. It's bikes and cars and sculpture. And everything's around for one simple reason: it's because I don't want to think I'm going to work every day. I want to feel like I should be here. Home is another place to sleep and take a shower, but I want to feel like I need to get back here, working. Every little thing that is here, I don't give a f--- what it is, it inspires me. It's here for a reason."

It's the dream garage that every car and bike nut in the world would have if only he had the space and could pony up the scratch to fill it up. "Pool tables, pinball machines, videogames, TV stereo—I want it just as comfortable as it is at home. And the same thing goes for the guys that work at West Coast Choppers. I don't want them to feel like they worked today. I mean f-----' Slayer played last night at *Monster Garage* and we all went over there and it was a private concert for twenty-five people with Slayer. What's cooler than that?"

Everyone who works at WCC is an enthusiast first and always. Ideas feed other ideas. Do what has not been done and respect the work are their credos.

"I have a whole wall of pictures, and I change them periodically. It's all my friends, friends who've died, bikes I've built in the past, cars that I like, shapes that I like, funny shit, and stuff like that. And I kind of gaze at it, and that's where my soul is. That's my inspiration. I don't know what to compare it to.

"A lot of people cruise down here and there's always some crazy stuff out in the parking lot. I dig it. I pull up sometimes and I'm pretty proud. I look at all of it happening and my chest fills up and I can't believe that all this is mine." The crowds keep coming back because the show is always changing. The free sideshow display of good stuff can include anything from wrestlers to movie stars to tail-draggin' '50 Mercurys. It really is anything goes.

Jesse's surreal life infects everything he comes in contact with. Witness the Four Corners area as a tourist destination. The constant line of visitors clutch their cameras, trying to get a glimpse into the work area, Cisco the dog keeping them at bay. "Is Jesse here?" "Where's Jesse?" "Is that Jesse?" All day long.

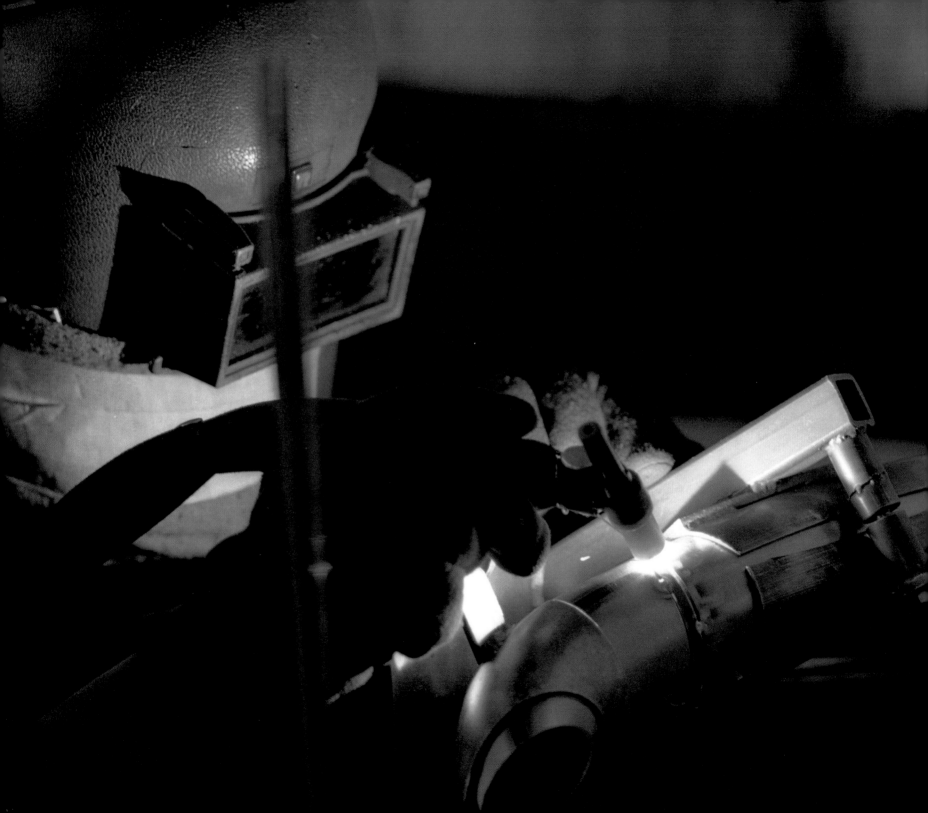

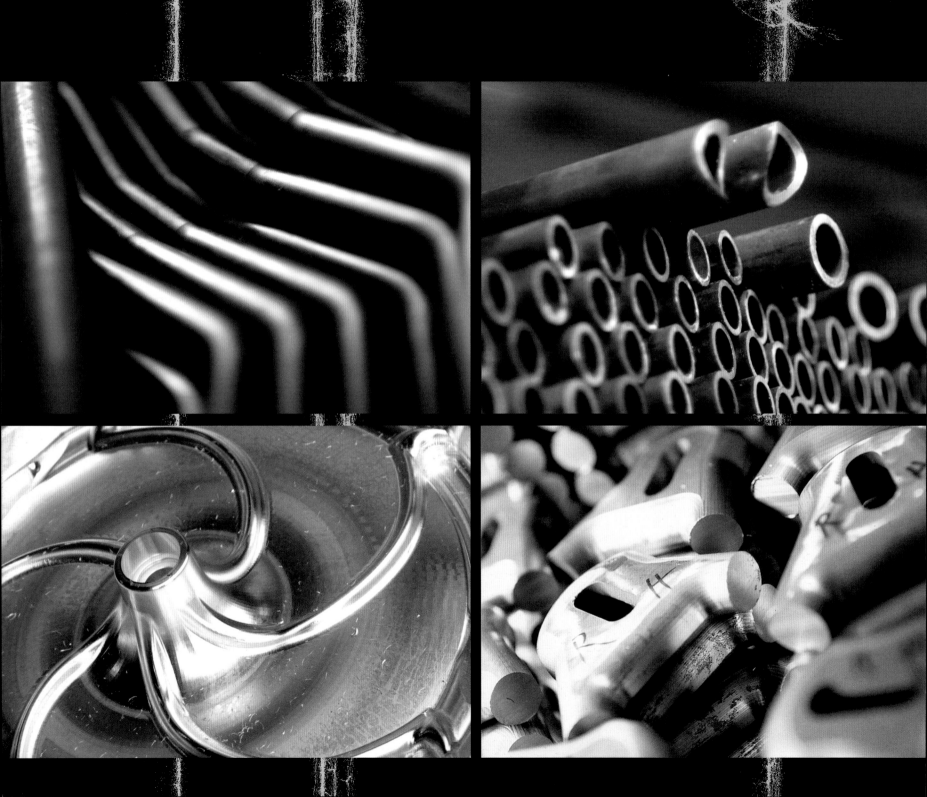

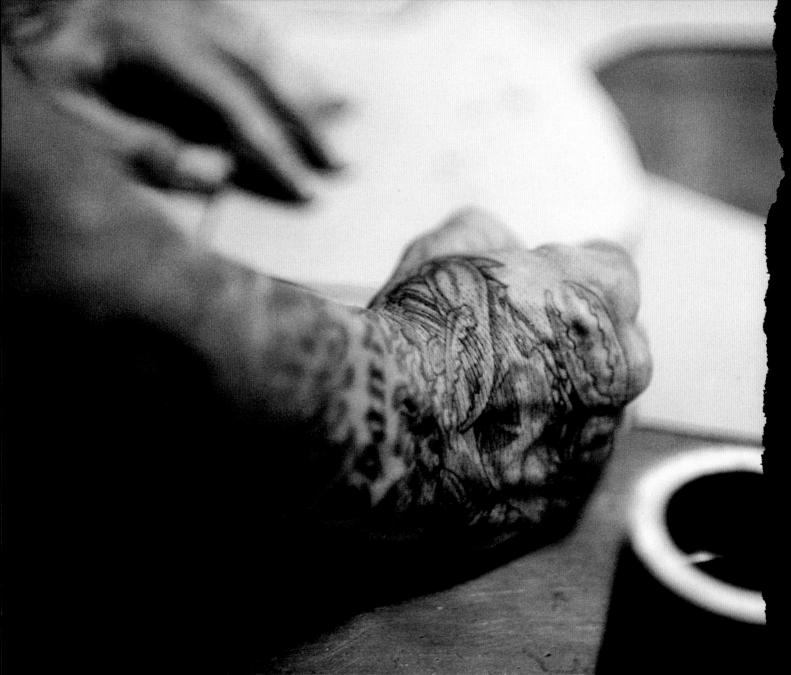

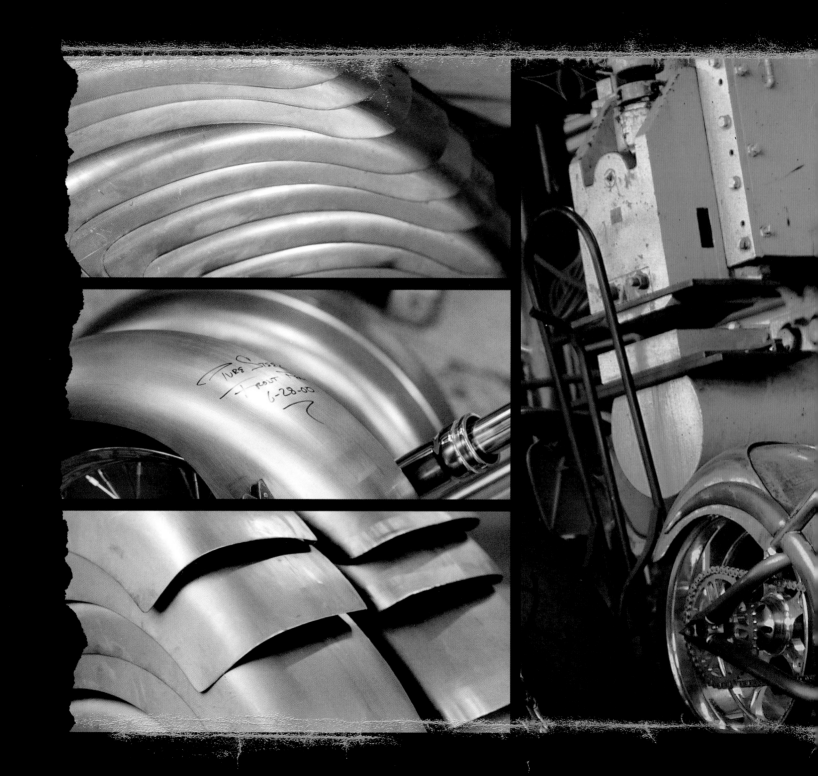

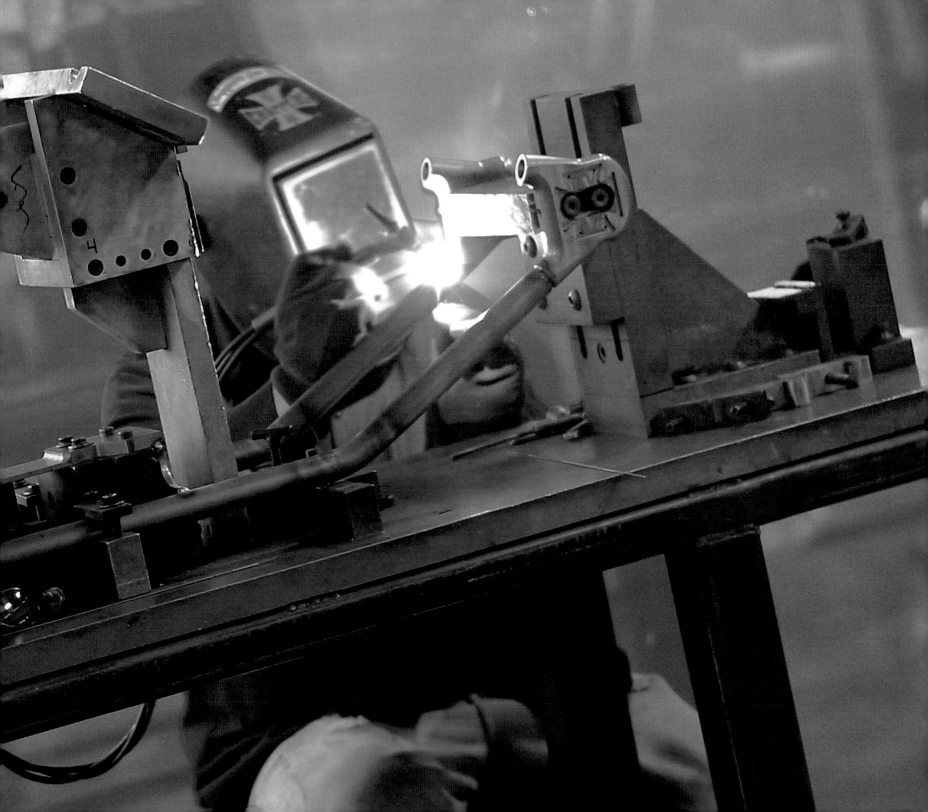

MEAN & CRUEL That's Our Rule!

Pay Up $ Sucker!

...ICAN MAFIA FULL OF HATE #?

COUNT·DOWN TO ECSTASY

got CHOPPERS ?

...I DON'T LIKE YOU 622 10?

HATE IS REALITY

JESSE WHO? www.chopperdogs.com

WARNING!
ALL FANCY LADIES
MUST CHECK IN WITH
THE SHIP'S DOCTOR
UPON BOARDING
THE CAPTAIN

LONG BEACH BUDDAH...

Complaint Dept.
CLOSED
There's the Door
MOTHERFUCKER

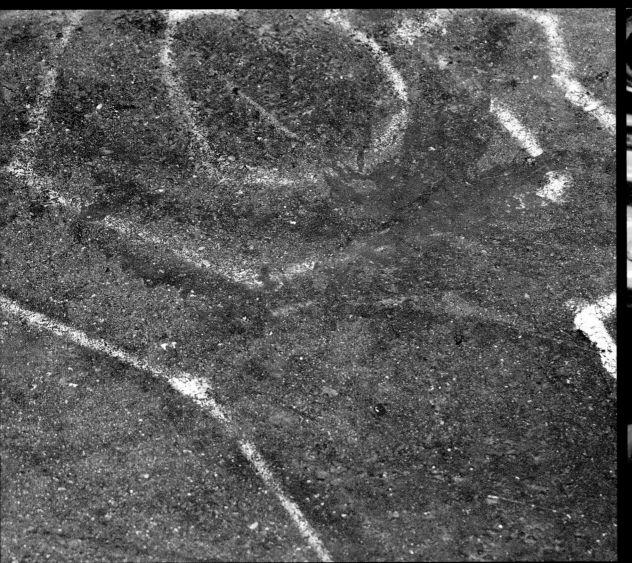

JESSE JAMES
"Head Chopper"

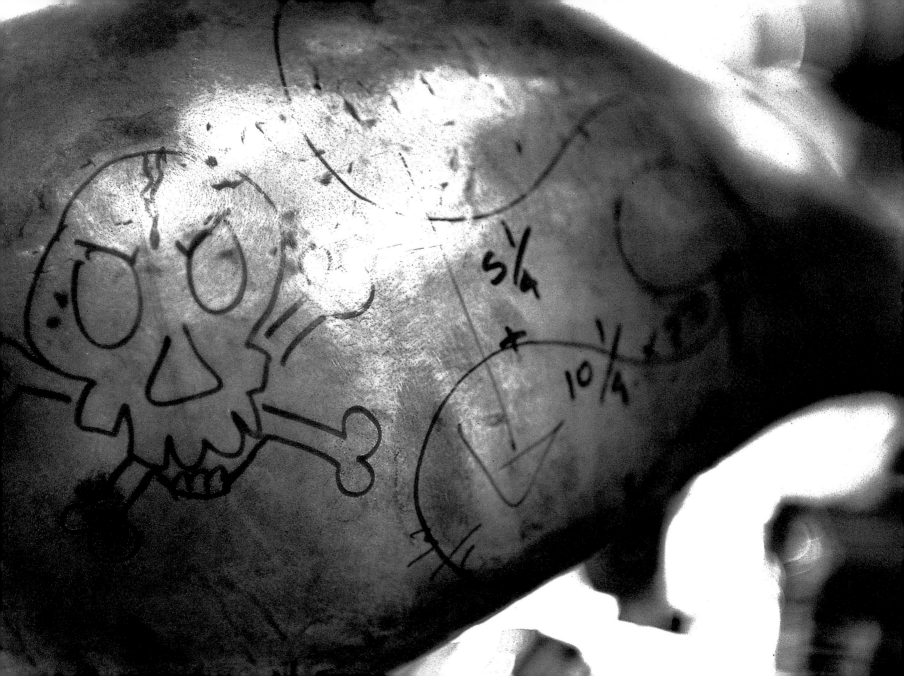

"*I don't do anything in my life that I don't want to do.*"

— J.J.

THE LIFE

That Jesse James, a foul-mouthed chopper builder, is now the most famous motorcycle personality ever is one of the bike world's great ironies. Chopper builders and riders are usually the outcasts of the motorcycle world and are never taken seriously by the major bike manufacturers. In the 1950s these troubled, menace-to-society bikers were said to represent only 1 percent of the biking population, and the 1 percenters were scorned by the general public and other bikers alike—most felt they gave the biking world a bad name.

Yet Jesse James has revitalized the world of custom bikes. He's Shaft and Von Dutch and Michelangelo rolled into one. He is courted by major automobile and motorcycle manufacturers. He has elevated his art to unforeseen heights and, at the same time, made the craftsman important and respected again. The biggest problem with Jesse is that he just won't do what anyone expects him to do. His lifestyle dictates that all lifestyles are rejected, including the one that bikers are supposed to lead. That pisses people off. He could be the ultimate independent. "Everybody hated me for a long, long f------ time and tried to steal my ideas and my employees. I've had at least thirty friends steal my ideas and swear that they were gonna put me out of business. I just keep my head down and do what I do."

The whole household-name, celebrity-joyride thing doesn't stick to his Dickies very well either. "In my circle, in Long Beach, there are still people who want to fight me every day. I've gotta watch my back around here. I'm right where I am, I'm where I've been my whole life and it keeps me pretty humble. But if I go up to, like, Alabama, they trip out. Suddenly, I'm a rock star."

Fame can make doors swing open and opportunity knock. But Jesse knows it's not a skill, that, in the end, it has no real value. "It's just a mathematical equation. It means that the number of people that know me is far greater than the number of people that I know. And that's it. It doesn't mean I'm greater or special or anything. It's just simple math."

Fame does sell a lot of T-shirts, and too many T-shirts can dilute the message. But for Jesse James, the big sellout isn't coming. "I think anyone else in my position would put out cheap pipe filler. You know, try to fill up that pipeline as full as possible. We're selling a lot of clothing, but as far as my end products—bikes, cars, and parts—I still want everything to be absolutely the best, and I'm coming up with the most f---- stuff I can think of. I'm doing frame kits now, to help a lot of other builders—guys like I was in my garage. I didn't have a lot of money, and I'd buy parts that didn't work or didn't fit, so it forced me to make my own stuff. But it would have been easier if I had had decent parts. A lot of people out there want to build their own bike in their garage, and they don't have the access to all the machines and knowledge I had. But as far as staying on the edge, I don't know. I just do whatever I want."

Still, his edge is sharp. "I haven't made it. I'm by far not where I want to be. I just feel like, you know, *next*? It's like doing the jet car on *Monster Garage*. I did it, I accomplished it. I just went 185 miles an hour in a car I built in five days and now it's on to the next more f------up hairball thing."

Seven-day weeks and eighteen-hour days on a television set can corrupt focus and distort purpose. Celebrity and the constant requests for time and appearances conspire to eat days and weeks at a time. Even with his well-known tenacity, Jesse can still feel the pull.

"You know, when I first got married, my wife made me take my Panhead out of the living room. Now I'm divorced again and the first thing I did in my new pad was put two bikes right in the f-----' living room. I just thought, 'You know, I need to get back to what I know.' And I need to wake up every day and see a motorcycle and that way I know what I'm supposed to be doing."

Being a rebel has always meant walking your own path, or in Jesse's case laying fifty feet of Pirelli Dragon rubber down your own path. The problem is that other people see the scorch marks and want to follow you.

"You know, there's a lot of stress, and when someone tells me I'm their hero, it's a pretty big task to live up to. But I try to live my life and work hard and do the TV show as best as I possibly can and do every bike as best as I possibly can to try and live up to everyone's expectations. It makes me want to work harder. I don't rest and say to myself, 'Hey, these people love me. I can do no wrong.' I just want to put the throttle to the floor and keep going and when they think they've seen everything, *wham!* I'll hit 'em with something else."

Adrenaline rush and the creative act may fuel his soul, but Jesse also feels the need to spark a flame in other people. He does it with the changes his bikes trigger in their owners and the spotlight focused on him as a media figure. "I think that the positive side of all this is that I use my TV show as a tool to teach kids and try to reach out to as many people as I can. I want to let parents know, Hey, buy your f-----' twelve-year-old a welder. Then he'll always have a twenty-five-dollar-an-hour job. If you send 'em to computer school, there's a million of those guys, you know, ready to jump out of a window because they don't have jobs. Teach 'em a trade. This country has gone so full force into dot-com stuff, every kind of funding that ever goes into schools is all for computers. Auto shops defunct everywhere."

The shop classes may be a low priority for school funding, but thanks to Jesse and *Monster Garage,* the classes are filling up for the first time in a generation. Kids get excited because they see Jesse on television construct something crazy, and they think, 'I know I could do that.' "Some shop teacher e-mailed me from back east telling me that if his kids work hard in class Monday through Thursday, then Friday they get to watch *Monster Garage* in class."

There's a couple of other kids who get to watch the metal-bending chopper hero up close. Jesse's daughter is too young to pick up a hammer just yet, but there's another Jesse James, with fire in his eyes and a welding torch in his hand. "I hope he wants to get into this, but I'm not gonna be one of those Little League dads and force anything on him. I want him to do whatever he wants to do. If he turns twenty and says 'Dad, I want to be a fashion designer or a stained-glass window maker, that's fine. This place will always be here for both of my children. I let them be here when they want to be, but I won't force it. My son, Jesse, is learning to weld and he's helping me shape and helping out the guys in the shop. I watch him do it and it's surreal because he looks exactly like me when I was his age. He's got the same intensity I had about taking things apart and then putting them back together. I can't think of anything cooler than having my son, who is also Jesse James, follow in my footsteps. Keep the steamroller rolling everybody into the ground."

It is said that having children changes everything. Suddenly, you have to set a positive example. You have to teach them right and wrong, even if right and wrong in your own life were a little bit indistinct at times. But kids are teachers, too. They can teach you to lighten up. They teach you how to have fun. They can help put years of anger and aggression into perspective. "This whole biker thing, I mean you go to Sturgis and everyone's standing around scowling and acting tough, and it's just, f--- that, I'm having fun. It's all about riding and just goofing off. This whole biker thing, you know, 'Live to ride, ride to live,' f--- that. I'll just put F--- YOU right on the side of the tank and keep rolling. So many people take it too serious, you gotta, like, be tough and stuff like that. I did that flathead chopper with Alfred E. Newman with a black eye on the tank, and it just says WORRY? in big letters."

To many riders the biggest appeal of motorcycles is that they're solitary vehicles. Whether for fun, escape, therapy, or just for the sheer thrill of it, nothing beats a speeding chopper. It is personal and pure and addictive and as the bikes get better and the motors get nastier it makes the rider wonder, Is there ever enough speed and power? What would make Jesse back off the throttle? "We've built some motors that are about as fast as you want to go. But I like to thrill myself, you know. I got a twin turbo Porsche that puts out 800 horsepower. I have a Suzuki that's got 300 at the rear wheel and the choppers put out 160 to 180 horsepower. And with that kind of power, if you can figure out a way to make it lighter and faster and quicker handling and stuff like that, it just enhances the ride even more."

Is Jesse James a 1 percenter? "Oh, I don't know. I'm just a good dad and a hard worker. I don't do anything in my life that I don't want to do." And Jesse's life, as rich and layered and exciting as it is, does not run on autopilot. At this point it's tempting to get complacent, but he stays hungry. "I stay scared. I wake up every day scared that this shit's gonna be like waterbeds—gone like that. And I'm never satisfied. Every bike I finish, I think, 'Oh, I should've done it like this, or I should've done that like that.' I'm still pushing myself with processes and techniques and skills. Like I learned how to be a coppersmith last summer and I made a whole bike out of copper with all mechanical joints."

Trust no one. Do it yourself. Hard work is the cure for everything. Success is self-inflicted. The Jesse James image is an easy one to buy into. Success on your own terms is the dream, but it's not all about telling everyone to f--- off just because you can.

"I think you have to define success first, what is successful for you. Success for me is to be able to come here and to work hard in peace and make beautiful stuff, and I don't have to do something I don't want to do. To not have to work on someone's bike that I don't like, just because I gotta pay my bills."

If there is any Jesse James–West Coast Choppers philosophy, it would probably sound something like this: Do what you want to do. Follow your own vision. Do good work. Be tenacious. Ignore the critics.

"It's like the old saying As hard as I'm trying to stay on top, there's twenty-five other motherf------ trying ten times harder to knock me off." No one enjoys triumph more than the underdog that digs his feet in and prevails. And he's not alone in the custom bike world.

"The ones that helped me along the way are relishing in it. Guys like Perewitz and Wink and guys like that, that always supported me. But the ones that were resistant, they're resentful because they had no part of my success.

"Everybody knows they're never gonna be Tom Cruise, they're never gonna be Jack Nicholson, never gonna be Jennifer Lopez. But everybody out there knows that they could be kinda like me. They could just practice and learn to weld really good and fabricate and make stuff and use kind of my philosophy and give people the finger and live life the way they want to and be happy. And I think people can relate to that. Everybody could be me."

Still, there's more to him than the self-deprecating tattooed Everyman. He is impossible to pin down and of course his greatest strength, that abrasive attitude, always provokes fierce opinions about Jesse James. He's a genius, he's a jerk, he's a folk hero, he's a hack, an angel, a godless corrupter.

"Let 'em talk. People can say whatever they want about me. I don't give a shit. I'm an easy target. I'm big. I've got tattoos, and, you know, I've got a big mouth. So they can think whatever they want to think."

To people living complicated lives, simplicity becomes the reward. "I jump into my '54 Chevy, stop, get something to eat, blasting home, seeing someone I know on the way home—one of my friends, dropping the ass end and throwing a bunch of sparks on him, and f-----' hauling ass. I mean, that's my life and it doesn't get better than that.

"All the bullshit and media stardom and TV and all that stuff, that'll all be gone someday. That ain't gonna last forever. But me, my shop, and my '54 Chevy, and my dog and my kids, that's what I love. That's the real Jesse James." West Coast Choppers is permanent. Cool transcends trend.

For once, the revolution was televised.

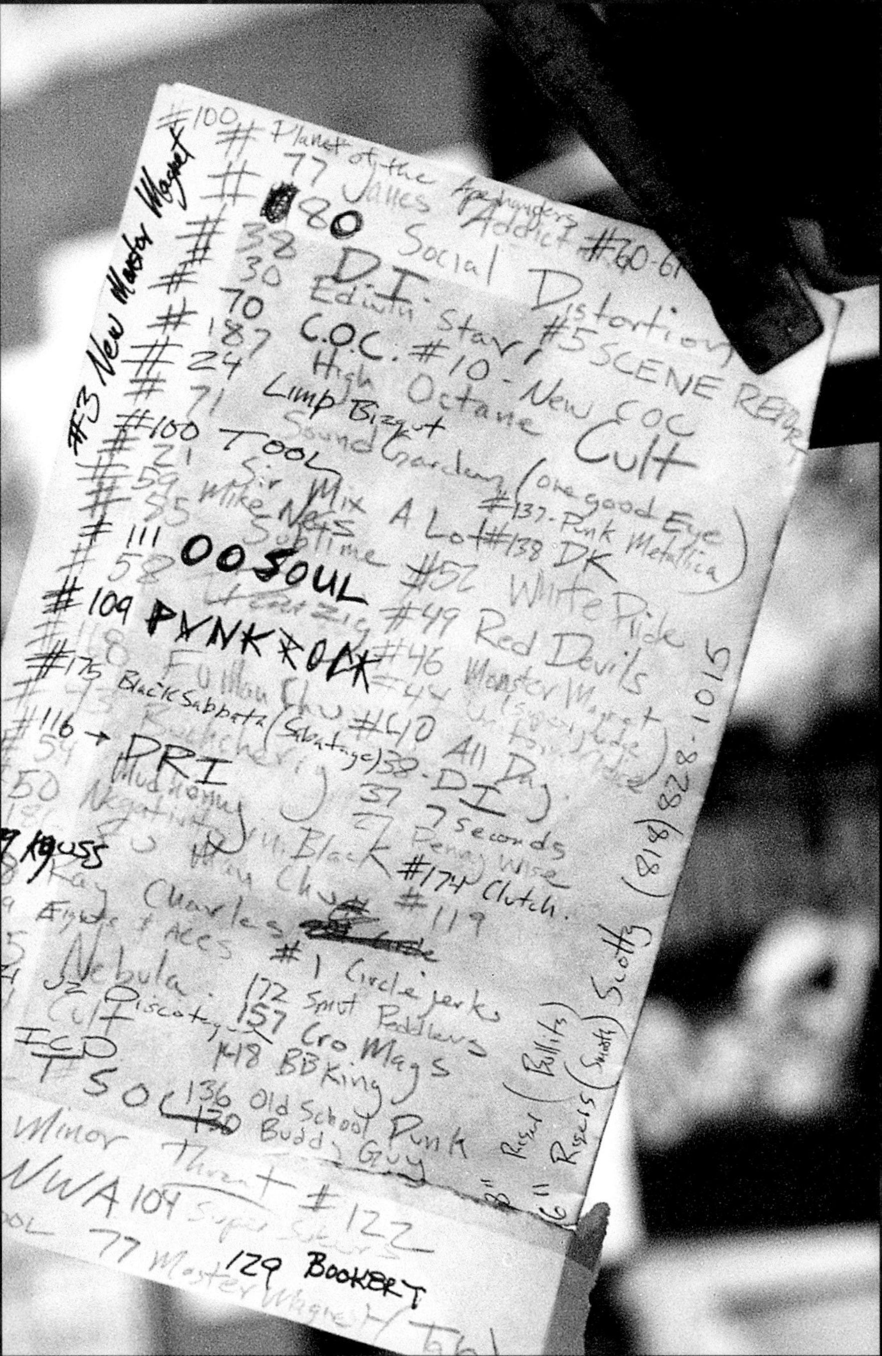

#3 New Master Magnet
Social Distortion
#5 SCENE REPORT
C.O.C. #10 - New COC
High Octane
Cult
Limp Bizqut
TOOL
Sir Mix A Lot #138 DK
#137 - Punk Metallica
Sublime
00 SOUL
#109 PUNK ROCK
#49 Red Devils
#46 Monster Magnet
#116 → PRI
37 7 seconds
#174 Clutch
Ray Charles
#1 Circle jerks
Nebula
172 Smut Peddlers
157 Cro Mags
148 BB King
136 Old School Punk
Buddy Guy
Minor Threat #122
NWA 104
129 BOOKERT
Scotty (818) 828-1015